# Notes from the Publisher

Welcome to a glimpse into the world of international quilting. At Stitch Publications our wish is for you to be able to explore beyond the boundaries of the country in which you live by experiencing and seeing what other fiber artists are doing.

In many countries, rather than learning from various books, quilters study under a single master, spending years progressing from simple techniques to the extremely difficult. Intricate designs are celebrated and sewing and quilting by hand is honored, and as such, hand quilting is the typical method used to quilt.

This book was written in its original language, Japanese, by a master quilter and artist, Yukari Takahara. We have done our best to make the directions easy to understand if you have some level of quilting experience, while maintaining the appearance and intent of the original author and publisher.

Much of this book is inspirational. By this we mean that there are not necessarily patterns for all the quilts you see in this book; rather it is a book to help you understand the process of designing and putting patterns together for your own story quilts.

We hope the beautifully designed handmade items in this book inspire and encourage you to make them for yourself.

## - Important Tips Before You Begin -

The following facts might suggest that intermediate or advanced quilters will be more comfortable working on these projects.

## - Techniques -

Beyond the "How to Appliqué " section (starting on p. 56), Ms. Takahara does not go into detailed descriptions of specific quilting, sewing or embroidery methods for each project. She assumes that the creator is familiar with sewing, quilting and embroidery techniques to some degree and thus relies heavily on the creator's ability to figure out the directions that are not specifically written out. It is advisable to understand the basics of appliqué, quilting, and embroidery if you are going to tackle designing your own story quilts.

## - Measurements -

There are no measurements given in this book.

## - Patterns/Templates -

The patterns given in the "Collection of Motifs & Designs" section at the back of the book were each used in various quilt vignettes that are seen throughout the book and are given as examples that you can use for your own quilts. You can use them at the size given in the book, or use a copy machine to shrink or magnify them to the size that you would like to have.

Stitch Publications, 2014

# Story Quilts - Through the Seasons

by Yukari Takahara

When walking through town  I sometimes stumble upon a place where I think to myself, "I love this shop!" If I'm feeling a little blue and stop by a bookstore, turning the pages of a picture book always makes me smile. When I walk into a shop that is selling soft and colorful yarn or fabric from all over the world, it makes me want to jump up and down with joy.

It was really thinking of all the things that I am passionate about that started my journey toward creating stories through quilts. Using fabric for my designs brings warmth to my creations much more so than just putting them to paper would ever do. Perhaps being surrounded by quilts is what continues to make me happy.

If you happened upon this book and turned the pages, you would have seen snippets and times in my life that I made into stories and depicted in my quilts. If that has inspired you to want to make your own story quilts, this book is for you.  It will bring me much joy if even just one person picks up a needle and thread and begins to create and tell their own unique stories through a quilt.

Yukari Takahara

 **Spring** 6

**Summer** 16

# CONTENTS

  26

Winter 36

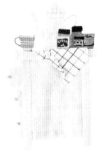

# Spring

## Gardening in the Sunshine

After the harsh cold of winter, plants begin to wake up with the coming of spring. Delicate leaves and stems appear where there were none the day before. Small buds in vivid colors that the force of nature creates so effortlessly herald the arrival of this valuable season.

Sunny Day

## Strolling Along

## Riding Through the Tulips

The season is awash with new discoveries and encounters of spring blooms. Tulips sway and seem to smile in the pleasant breeze making me want to follow the smell of spring as I ride along. I am happy that I am still quite a ways from home.

Off to School

## The Bookmobile is Here!

The bookmobile, laden with books, comes once a month and stops under a large tree. A child dashes over to see what is new, while another one who can't make up his mind calls his older sister over to ask for help. Even the leaves on the trees and the forest animals want to join in the excitement as springtime has come to the mountains.

## Visiting the Newborn Foal

One never tires of seeing evidence of a new life. A newborn foal whose mother stands guard and watches with a gentle gaze. Living in the city, it is not something that I often get to see.

A Garden Wedding

Girls on a Sunny Day

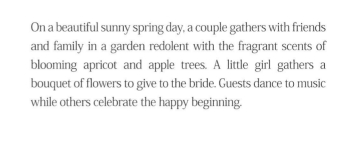

On a beautiful sunny spring day, a couple gathers with friends and family in a garden redolent with the fragrant scents of blooming apricot and apple trees. A little girl gathers a bouquet of flowers to give to the bride. Guests dance to music while others celebrate the happy beginning.

# Summer

### Inside on a Rainy Day

The flowers appear to thoroughly enjoy the warm shower of rain as I look through the window while playing with my dolls.

Running through the almost deserted amusement park on a rainy day makes another boring day full of fun.

### Carousel Rides in the Rain

## My Favorite Redwork

Summer is the perfect time of year to do something by one's self or travel to new places that one hasn't experienced before. It is a season filled with adventure. Even if you go so far as across the sea, you will always see your mother's arms welcoming you home.

## My Little Boat (Mon Petit Bateau)

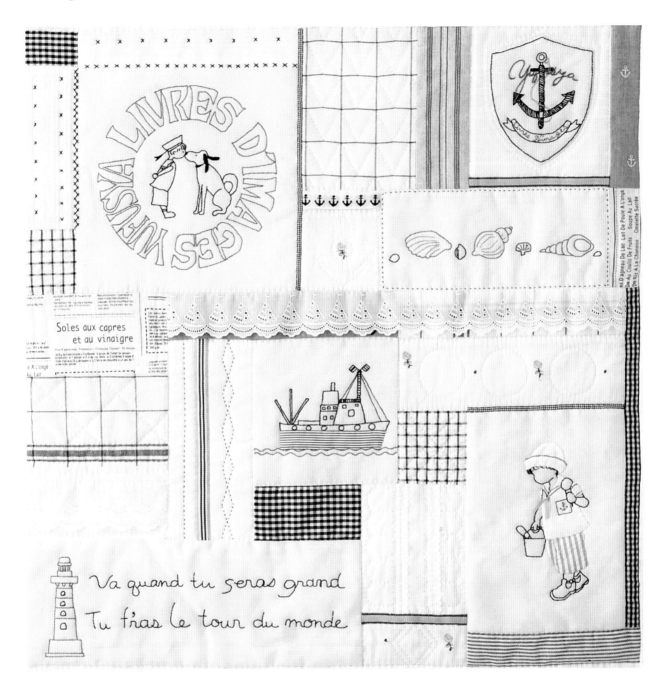

Summer Vacation

It is fun to play outside in the summer sunshine surrounded by yellow sunflowers and red holly-hocks stretching high above their green leaves.

Stripes...gingham...polka dots...summer brings carefree children running and playing in the sparkling sun wearing colorful patterned clothes.

Kids in the Summer

(facing page)

## Little Yu's Bedroom

I love spending time in my bedroom with the lace curtains, white bed, and floral wallpaper. It's filled with the things I love from childhood like my dolls and my teddy bear that I can't do without.

## Paddington Station

Paddington Station in London bustles with activity as people head out to various destinations. Tickets are bought, passengers are dropped off by taxis, and last minute souvenirs are packed into bags while everyone hurries on board the trains.

# Autumn

## Gifts of Autumn

Fall appears suddenly one day with scent of dried grass and colorful leaves falling in the sharp wind.

## Memories

Reflecting...steam rising from a warm cup of cafe au lait...

Huddling together and sharing warmth on an oversize chair...

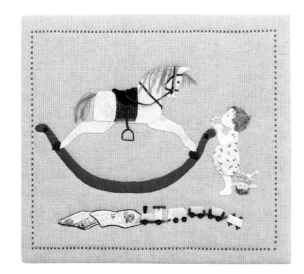

## My Brother's Rocking Horse

## Can You Fix Mine Too?

I always want to have my favorite dolls and toys around me. If we had an older brother who would gladly fix anything that was broken, they would last forever. Wouldn't it be wonderful to have a place like this full of things to play with? Toys are lined up on the shelves waiting to be chosen. Dolls eagerly await their turn to be chosen too.

## Picnic Under the Tree

Throw on your warm clothes and come outside! There's nothing quite like enjoying a picnic of apple pie and cinnamon swirls while sitting on a blanket on top of dried leaves.

Our Special Spot

## Walking Together

A group of friends, showing their personalities through gestures, hairstyles, and clothing, walk along together on their way home from school.

## Autumn Leaves in Town

Rural villages in England often look like they belong in picture books. The houses, of different styles and eras, are nestled together. Honey-colored stone walls and ivy-covered lattice windows give off a sense of warmth and togetherness.

## Promenade

As the leaves on the large Zelkova trees begin to alter in color, the air subtly shifts with the changing season.  Sitting near the trees and relaxing at an outdoor cafe while people-watching, you happily dwell on the beauty of the day.

My Dolls

Sunday Afternoon

The warmth of the fireplace and the delicious smell of a cake baking fill the house. Secret treasures can be found in the attic, like the dollhouse my Mother had from her childhood. Beautifully patterned china fills the hutch and reminds us that it is time for Sunday afternoon tea.

Winter
37

## New Friends?

Christmas comes closer with every turned page of the calendar. There is excitement about the coming holiday and perhaps a little worry about gifts not arriving on time. But most of all Christmas is a time to celebrate and for people all over the world to wish for peace on earth.

## Getting Ready for Bed

Presents from Santa

Fireside

If you look closely, every snowflake that falls is completely unique in its shape. The one thing that is similar about all snowflakes is how cold they are to the touch. On a snowy day, the most wonderful place to be is inside a warm house sitting next to a fireplace with the fire crackling and popping in the background.

It's Still Snowing

A Snowy Night

Heading Home

Village in the Snow

Large, fluffy snowflakes begin to fall from the sky as darkness descends. Snow accumulates on the church spire and the roofs of the houses large and small. One by one lights come on and spill from the windows as the village settles down for the night under a blanket of new snow.

# Where My Story Quilts Are Created

Drop by my home, studio, and shop, Yuufu-sha , in Aioi City, Hyogo Prefecture

I've always wanted to live a life that is rich. To me, richness is not found in the abundance of information or the collection of things. Rather, it comes through doing what I love each season in a wonderful location; using my imagination, my eyes, and  hands to create beauty through pictures and stories from fabric. That is how this place, Yuu-fu-sha, which means "where the gentle wind blows," came to be.

# Welcome to my Home, Studio, and Shop

When I opened my doors fourteen years ago, I envisioned a place where anyone of any age or lifestyle could come and feel relaxed and at home.

Wondering what kind of customers will stop by, I make sure that the window displays are welcoming.

Many treasures have been added to the garden over the ten years including this bird bath where birds come to get refreshed.

Most customers drive to my shop so I added cute little welcoming decorations to each parking spot.

The moss-covered bricks in the path were carefully placed one by one.

There is a feeling of excitement as one grasps the antique doorknob to open the door to the book gallery.

The various found objects situated around the garden are exposed to the elements and add a rustic quality.

My husband and I had a dream that we could build a life together that was rich in creativity and ingenuity far from our hectic lives. Leaving the bright lights of the city as well as my job as an art teacher, we settled in my husband's hometown. I began to build a business around creating things and teaching others all the things I loved to do...an intriguing variety of handicrafts, painting, picture book gallery, shop and cafe. This unlikely collection of my interests was the birth of my studio and shop called Yuufu-sha .

I believe strongly that everyone can foster a deep appreciation of life at its fullest if they are surrounded by wonderful opportunities to grow and learn in a richly creative environment. As a teacher, I sought to impart these things in my new venture.

Initially, advertising was word of mouth as people who had an interest in books and handicrafts stopped by. Clearly they were flooded by warm feelings and a calming sense of nostalgia when they were here; confirming my desire to offer a space where one could relax in a positive state of mind and heart.  I planted flowers and bushes that bloom over the four seasons to soften the worn building and rustic exterior. I experienced customers' imaginations stirring as they spent time here. My dream truly is the gentle breeze upon the soul that I envisioned.

# Picture Books Inspire My Imagination

Picture books have always brought joy to me. They are fun, inspire happiness, and were no small part of sparking my dream.

Long before I opened Yuufu-sha, my husband and I had begun collecting picture books. Over the years our collection had steadily climbed to where we had over 1200 books. In one section of our shop, we have all of our picture books out on display for our customers to browse through and read while they are having tea.

As a child I looked at and read my picture books over and over, fascinated by how the author or illustrator depicted landscapes, cityscapes, and animals and of places and things that I had never experienced in person. I learned so much from them and my mind would spin with possibilities. You can see how picture books influenced my appliqué and quilting projects. When I teach appliqué to my students, I often have them choose designs they like from picture books.

## Favorite Authors and Books

The settings of the stories as well as the expressions of the children, which are so wonderfully depicted, are some of the reasons these books are among my favorites (top). Brian Wildsmith's books with his amazing illustrations of wildlife makes him a favored choice (bottom).

## Bookseller in Hay-on-Wye

Three years ago I had the privilege of visiting Hay-on-Wye, a small town in Wales on the English border. They are known for their books and booksellers. I have wonderful memories of time flying by as I spent hours and hours looking through old picture books.

The books are sometimes classified by their country of origin (a); or by specific themes (b). The high ceilings and soft light make for a comfortable place to settle in and read in the book gallery (c).

# My Studio

One of my favorite forms of self-expression is to use cloth as my canvas - take my needle and thread and little by little bring a story to life.

Even with the cares of day-to-day life nipping at my heels, I always finish one epic quilt for the class exhibition each year. Drawn sketches on pieces of paper eventually become part of the whole. I transfer these to cloth and appliqué and embroider the designs to bring the quilt to completion.

My passion and creativity are unleashed when I work in my studio. My quilts almost always depict casual everyday kinds of vignettes of life seen throughout the year. Nostalgic scenes are shown by texture and color that are full of movement. I do a lot of appliqué work than can appear to be complex, but I tend to use very simple embroidery stitches. Sometimes I add beads or other embellishments. I think that the uniqueness of my designs really come from things like the facial expressions on the people, leaves on trees or even nuances like different ways to create hair, scarves or hats. Each little decision made as I work bring the quilts to life.

## Fabric & Scrap Stash

I keep my scraps as they are almost always usable in a new project.

How you choose to organize, whether by color or design, is purely a personal choice.

## Notions & Tools

Colored pencils and crayons are what I use on my sketches to bring them to life before transferring the designs to cloth.

I put my tools in cute baskets on my desk to keep everything organized.

Stuffed animals, ribbons and such sit lined up on the top of my storage chest.

The various collected items I use for specific appliqué projects are kept handy in one place.

# My Organized Kitchen

My life requires extreme efficiency. With being so busy I am even more determined to use each moment of each day wisely finding time to do the things I love. This includes how much time I spend in the kitchen each morning whipping up meringue for the cakes.

I love my old, battered copper kettle of more than ten years.

So that I can do other things while whipping the egg whites, I set up the bowl on an upside down lid to hold it in place while the hand mixer is held steady by a can.

The lampshade, made with handmade lace, hanging from the ceiling light has little animals appliquéd on it.

I made the curtains out of gingham and the tie-backs are embroidered with little designs.

The corner of the kitchen also serves as the dining room. I have decorated the walls with little pieces of art and handmade things.

My measuring cups are within easy reach on the window sill that also holds my glass bottle collection.

It might seem that with our desire to live a simple but rich life we could relax more, but the reality is that I have to be very structured about my time. I make breakfast at 6:30 a.m. and bake pastries and treats for the cafe. Lunch is at noon; afternoon tea at 3 p.m. with dinner at 6 p.m. I find comfort in the old and new and love my kitchen with the old white tiled counters, my scorched oven mitts, antique scale, and old copper pot.

# My Shop and Cafe

In 2006 I decided to expand further than our gallery and classroom to allow even more people to come by. The next chapter became the opening of our shop and cafe.

An antique stained glass window (a); hooks for customers' bags (b); old bricks from England that add to the ambiance (c); kits available for sale on our website (d).

Our dream that started out rather small has grown over the years. My husband, who has always supported me behind the scenes, took an active part in our new venture and did much of the work. We extended the building to house the cafe which we called "livre d'images" (picture book in French). Antique and found items collected over the years were incorporated into the interior and exterior of the addition. We wanted a brighter and different feel than the Tudor of the original building so we made it lighter.

We have our cafe set up with little tables like they do in Paris; tea time with cake and pastries.

Our reliable and wonderful staff help run the cafe, shop, and website. All the open space makes it easy for them to communicate throughout the day (e); even our powder room shows our attention to detail with the lighting and other fixtures (f).

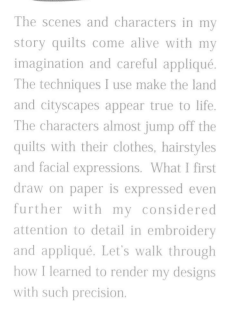

# How to Appliqué

The scenes and characters in my story quilts come alive with my imagination and careful appliqué. The techniques I use make the land and cityscapes appear true to life. The characters almost jump off the quilts with their clothes, hairstyles and facial expressions. What I first draw on paper is expressed even further with my considered attention to detail in embroidery and appliqué. Let's walk through how I learned to render my designs with such precision.

**Notions & Tools You Will Need to Begin**

Tracing paper, heavyweight paper for templates, light table, Chaco paper or other chalk-based pattern transfer paper, ballpoint pen, pencil, scissors, background fabric (what you will appliqué onto), batting, fabric scraps or fat quarters for your appliqué pieces, embroidery floss, needles, ribbon, yarn, or other materials for embellishments.

*Lesson*

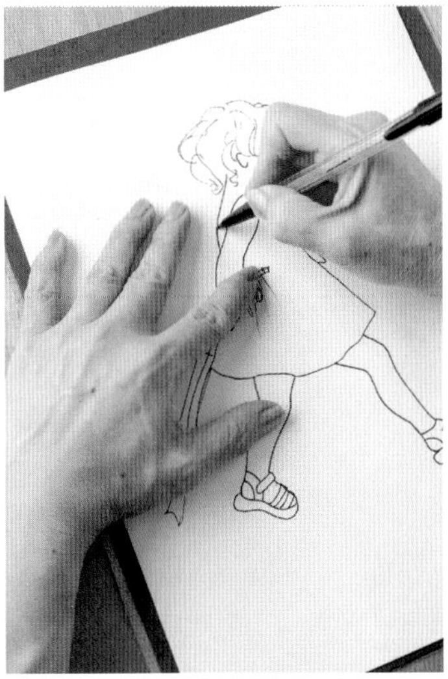

1 Place the background fabric right side up on a flat surface. Lay the Chaco paper (or other chalk-based pattern transfer paper) on top (chalk side down) of the background fabric with the appliqué design on the top. Using a ballpoint pen, trace the entire design. Once the design has been transferred to the background fabric, lay it on top of a piece of batting; baste them together.

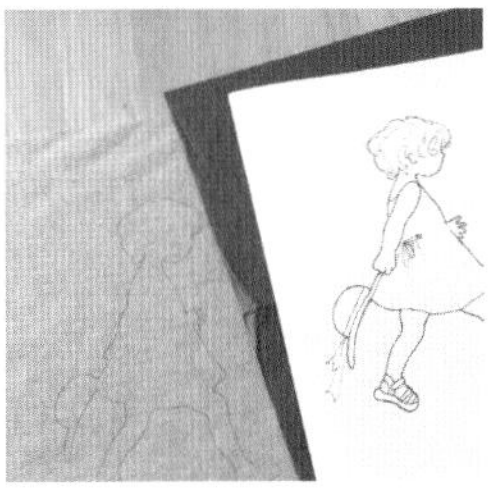

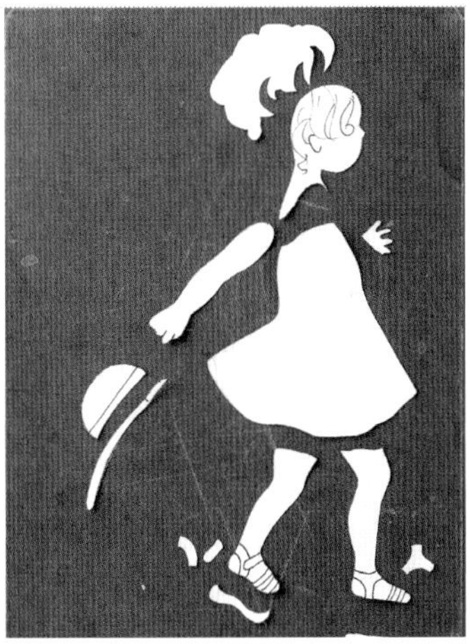

2 Using a light table (or a window on a bright day) transfer the design from the original paper to the heavyweight paper. Cut each area apart that will be a different piece of the design. If the clothes call for pleats or gathering, make the template big enough to accommodate for that process. I cut out each entire piece even if another piece will be layered on top of it.

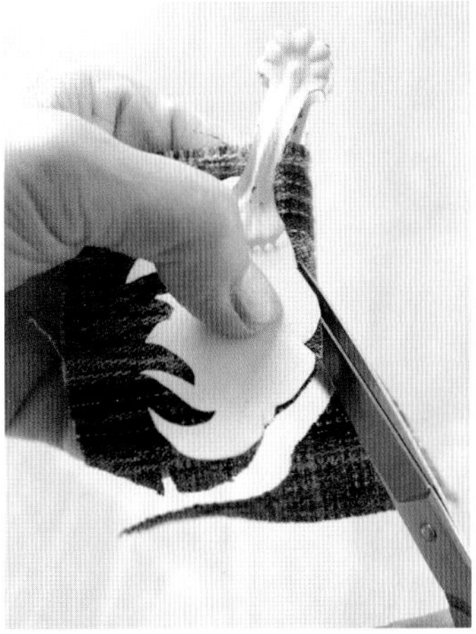

3 Cut out the appliqué piece for the hair without any seam allowance. I think it looks more realistic when the edges fray a little bit. The effect is particularly interesting when it is a loosely woven fabric.

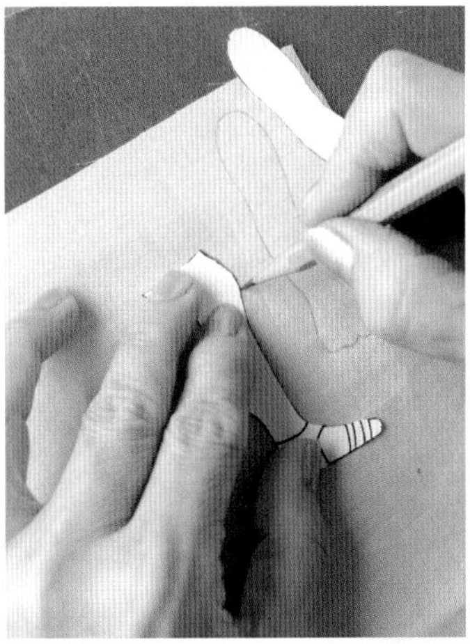

4 Take each individual piece of the design that you will be appliquéing onto the background piece and place on the fabric that you choose. Using a sharpened pencil, trace around the appliqué patterns.

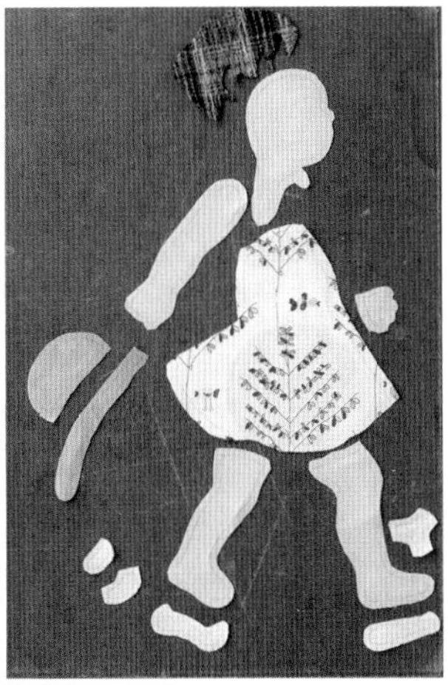

5 Add a 0.5 cm [¼"] seam allowance to each piece. If a piece is extremely tiny, add only 0.3 cm [⅛"] seam allowance around the curves.

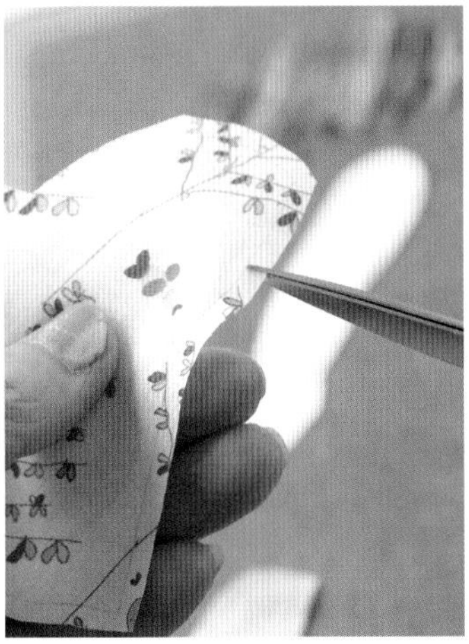

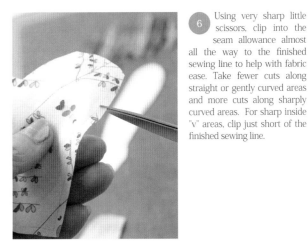

6 Using very sharp little scissors, clip into the seam allowance almost all the way to the finished sewing line to help with fabric ease. Take fewer cuts along straight or gently curved areas and more cuts along sharply curved areas. For sharp inside "v" areas, clip just short of the finished sewing line.

**7** Begin by appliquéing the face, left hand, legs and soles of the sandals. Lay each piece on top of the design that was transferred onto the background fabric. Turn the seam allowances under as you appliqué each piece down, being careful to just cover the marked lines so they cannot be seen. Make sure you start by appliquéing the pieces in order and appliquéing the next ones on top. You do not need to appliqué down areas that will be covered by a piece to keep the thickness at a minimum.

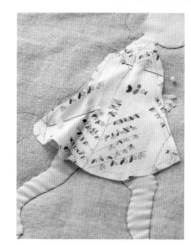

**8** Next you will appliqué the dress. Use pins to hold the gathers or tucks in place while you appliqué around the edges. Appliqué the right arm in place. Use the tip of your needle to tuck the seam allowance under as you work. Sometimes it will help to use your fingernail from your other hand to hold the appliqué in place as you do this.

**9** While it depends on what kind of fabric or material you are using for the hair, it can be fun and interesting to leave the edges unfinished with no seam allowance. Blindstitch around the perimeter. If the edges are fraying too much to blindstitch the outer edges, you can carefully take stitches into the background fabric anywhere in the hair, trying to make the thread disappear in the woven threads.

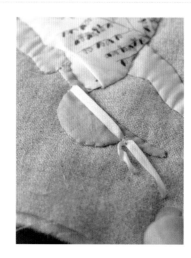

**10** Appliqué the hat down making it appear that she is carrying it in her hand. Then use a ribbon or other embellishment to finish the hat.

**11** Appliqué the sandal straps that go over the ankle and heel area. To make the straps across the front of the foot, stitch them using three strands of embroidery floss and an Outline Stitch.

**12** Add a little tied bow to the dress with four strands of embroidery floss

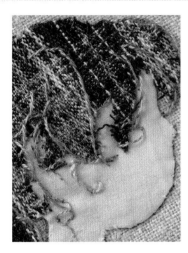

13. To give the hair even more dimension, use one strand of embroidery floss in a color that will blend in with the overall hair color. Loosely stitch it down using an outline stitch. You can also cut the strands of floss slightly longer than where you want them to end; curl and manipulate them to look like hair and stitch down a couple of places along the length to hold it in place.

14. The three-dimensional aspects of the hair and dress, as well as the lifelike curve of the arms and legs, help to make the little girl come to life.

Lesson

# Variations of the Same Pattern

The look of your final design will depend completely on the choices you make when it comes to color, fabrics, and the balance of embroidery stitching in comparison to the appliquéd fabric pieces. I want you to look at the patterns on the next few pages. Notice that I am using the same basic patterns, but getting very different portrayals of the little girls. You can use different color floss, cottons, wools, or other embellishments to create the look you want for your project.

A summer version of the little girl has her wearing a one-piece bathing suit. Stitching out the shape of her body allows for subtle emphasis of the arms and legs.

By using wool and woven fabric, the look has transformed to a winter scene. Notice that you can add additional design effects when you are also choosing background fabrics. In this case, I chose a fabric with tiny white dots that reminded me of snowflakes.

I've embroidered the little girl's outline, but added fullness to the dress along with three-quarter length sleeves. A flower in one hand and a teddy bear in the other completes yet another unique design. It is fun to exchange what the little girl is carrying depending on the overall quilt theme you are working on.

Even doing the simplest of applications by using mostly embroidery along with the appliqué technique used only for the dress and hat, make an interesting variation.

In this example I chose to have similar colors for both the embroidery as well as the color in part of the dress. It appears fresh and reminds me of summer. The hair is sewn down with raw edges (no seam allowance to turn under) showing and enhanced with embroidery on top.

If you want to emphasize certain colors or techniques, make them stand out more than others. I stitched the girl's body, hair, and canteen using a simple embroidery stitch, then created fullness in the appliquéd red-checked dress and backpack.

The little girl in this pattern appears to be begging, pointing, or asking for something. It was fun to create a winter version and a summer version simply by my different choice of materials for the clothes that matched the season.

See how the trousers on the little winter girl make it seem to be a very different pattern than when exposing her legs by appliquéing them in the summer version? Whether or not you choose to add facial features is up to you, but even without them on the little summer girl, you get the sense of her expression coming through.

# Alternatives for Hair and Hairstyles

I have found that using a plain black or brown fabric to depict hair can make it appear too flat and two-dimensional. To really add interest to hair, try to imitate delicate textures and things like how light or wind would affect the hair. In order to have the hair not look like a wig, I use a raw edge technique with no seam allowance. Stitch down the hair and add texture by embroidering on top of the base fabric.

### Finely-woven Woolen Plaids

### Tiny Patterned Prints

Of course, it all depends on the size of your character, but typically it is best to use small prints, finely-woven plaids, or tiny stripes when choosing fabric for hair. Think about the nuances of color that you want to come through and how that will interact with the rest of your character's clothing and overall theme.

### Miniscule Stripes

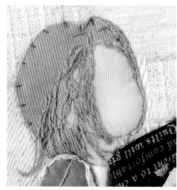

### Embroidery Stitches

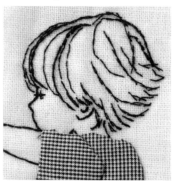

If I want my project or character to appear lighter or less busy, I will use embroidery for the head and hair. You can choose to use multiple colors if you like, although I like the look of one color. It is easy to get natural-looking hair with embroidery stitches.

### Hairstyles that are Visible Under Hats

Hats are a great way to add interest to the characters and are particularly useful to help differentiate seasons. Rather than drawing out the hair on the background exactly, I decide whether or not I should add a hair base with fabric or just use embroidery. It is fun to randomly add the hair under the hats.

# Depicting a Variety of Clothes

One of the best ways to convey seasons in my story quilts is through my characters' clothing. I like to be very detailed when it comes to fabric and design choices by doing such things as adding fullness or pleats to dresses and skirts, knits or tiny florals or stripes to get the overall effect.

## Skirts

It is amazing how much a simple technique, such as gathering or pleating fabric, can make to the character in your story quilt. Cut the fabric for the skirts larger than the final area; add the gathers and pleats; and baste before you begin to appliqué the fabric down.

## Knits for Sweaters

Microscopic cross-stitching can be perfect for sweaters (top); using an Outline Stitch and embroidery floss in several colors makes the stripes for the turtleneck (middle); knit socks are great for sweaters. I like to keep them on hand (bottom).

## Hats & Scarves

Use your imagination and items you might have on hand. I cut up an old pair of finely-knit socks for the knit cap. To make the scarf, I used embroidery thread and knit it on some bamboo skewers I had in my kitchen.

Because the characters in my quilts are often quite small, I like to use very tiny or small prints that work well proportionally. I have found that the Liberty of London prints work well for this.

## Tiny Prints for Clothes

# Additional Embellishments

When doing appliqué, it is relatively easy to choose cotton fabrics that make the most sense for the given design. However, to bring forth the most realism in my characters and other designs in my quilts, I find that incorporating other materials and embellishments can add depth. Hemp and wool add texture, while other materials bring out little touches that add enjoyment to my work.

## Hemp or Fine Twine

## Lace & Organdy

Just a little bit of cut-work lace can be a treat to the eye. Organza, or other sheer fabric, is perfect to depict glass or a lampshade.

I often use coarse hemp or woven hemp cloth to make baskets or straw hats as the texture is perfect for such designs. Depending on what I am trying to portray, I might also use them for flooring or a road.

## Cotton Prints with Script

It's fun for me to collect fabric along the way that has words written on it. They work great for things like picture books, sketch books, billboards, posters and signs. I keep them organized by size of the script so that I can find the right size to match the proportions I need.

## Corduroy & Felted Wool

Corduroy is a wonderful fabric to add dimension to a design. I've used it in the tail and mane of the toy horse and the bellows for a fireplace. Felted wool gives a sense of warmth that is fun to use for pets or winter outerwear. Even materials such as fuzzy wool can be a fun look, which I used for a little stuffed animal.

## Beads

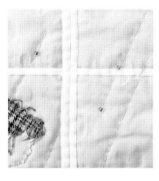

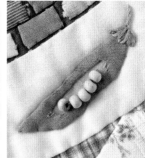

There is an endless selection of beads available. They are an excellent choice to represent raindrops on a window, part of a baby rattle, or peas.

## Buttons

## Ribbon

Ribbons are an obvious choice of embellishment that I use often. Try different techniques such as tying them down or making them appear to float to add dimension to your project.

Like beads, there are a myriad of styles, sizes, and colors of buttons, buttons and more buttons. For any part of your patterns that are round, try to see if a button would make the design more interesting and playful.

## Miscellaneous Items

To make these tiny little knitting needles, I glued microscopic round wooden beads to the ends of a couple of toothpicks.

## Cording

Leather or synthetic cording comes in many colors and diameters. Sometimes it can be the perfect material to represent part of your design...such as for a watering can handle or knitting needles.

# Enhancements Using Handwork

Last, but not least, the background fabric that I use is critical to the overall effect of my story quilt. Whether a city or landscape, I don't usually choose a large plain piece of cloth that has no pattern as it can make the design fall flat. Choose backgrounds that complement your appliqué designs, the season, or other emotions that you want to evoke.

I love the challenge of adding trees to my quilts. Once the trunk is appliquéd on, the leaves can be added in any number of ways using various techniques and materials for different effects. I sometimes use a Chain Stitch or Straight Stitch with embroidery floss to show young leaves. Ribbon embroidery adds texture and makes wonderful fall leaves, as do tiny little cut raw edge pieces that are sewn down. The level of detail you incorporate can really add to your quilt.

## Trees

   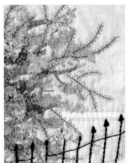 

## Flowers & Leaves

It's not as easy for me to add expression to flowers and plants as it is to people, but it is still possible. I think about the characteristics of each type of flower and use techniques and materials to enhance them. I almost always use some combination of fabric, embroidery stitches and/or ribbon embroidery to get the desired look.

## Roofs & Building Materials

I visualize typical houses and buildings as can be seen in villages of rural England. It is so much fun to design my own little village. The choices for siding, doors, roofs, or other building materials are endless, so do not make your buildings too much the same or monotonous.

## Snow

 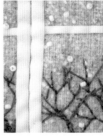 

Snow can be expressed in many ways. I do so with sequins, beads or embroidery depending on what technique I think will look best with my overall design.

*Lesson*

# Collection of Motifs & Designs

CONTENTS

All the motifs and designs on the following pages have been used in the quilts in this book and are examples that you can use when creating your own story quilts. You are encouraged to draw or trace your own patterns for things that you want to depict in your quilts. Feel free to use these as a guide and change them to suit your purposes.

p. 14 - Girls on a Sunny Day

p. 21 - Kids in the Summer

p. 21 - Kids in the Summer (alternate)

p. 21 - Kids in the Summer

p. 21 - Kids in the Summer

p. 19 - Feeling Nautical

p. 5 - Getting Ready

p. 28 - My Brother's Rocking Horse

p. 5 - Strolling in the Winter

p. 4 - Picnic

p. 5 - Pancakes for Breakfast

p. 37 - Sunday Afternoon

p. 27 - Memories

p. 29 - Can You Fix Mine Too?

p. 22 - Little Yu's Bedroom

p. 29 - Can You Fix Mine Too?

p. 37 - Sunday Afternoon

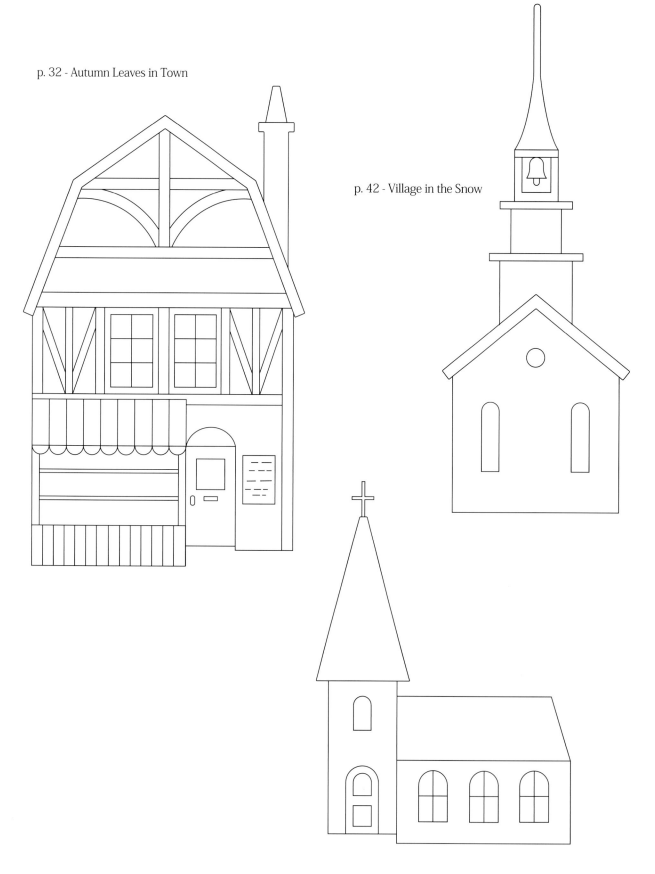

p. 32 - Autumn Leaves in Town

p. 42 - Village in the Snow

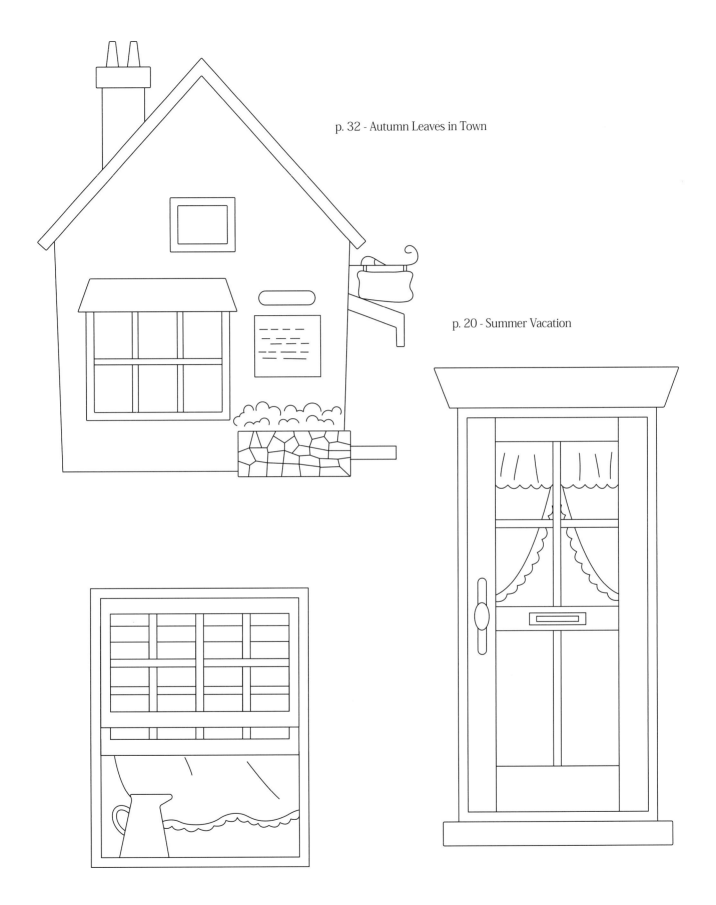

p. 32 - Autumn Leaves in Town

p. 20 - Summer Vacation

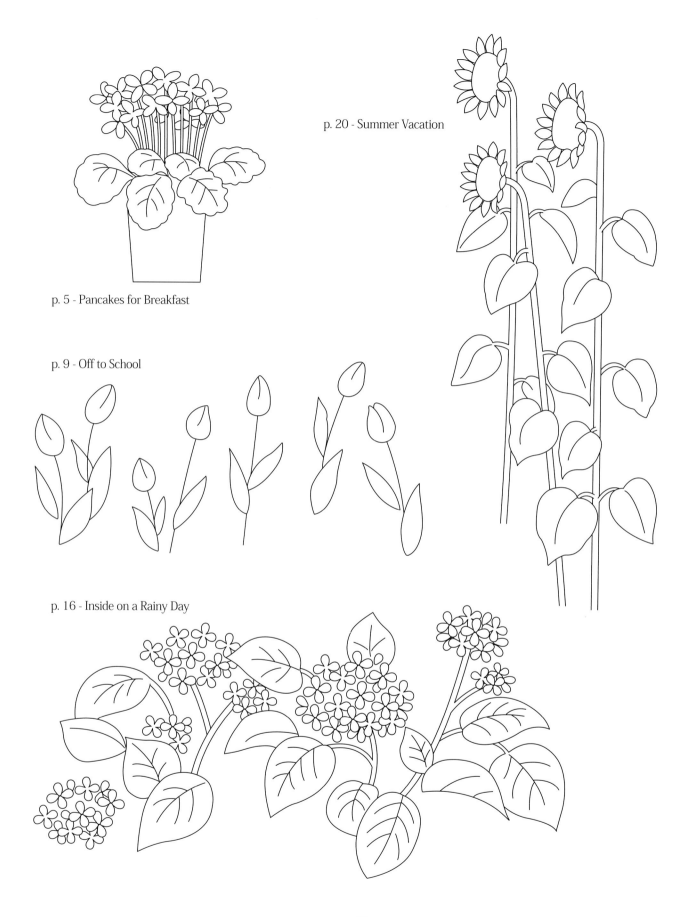

p. 20 - Summer Vacation

p. 5 - Pancakes for Breakfast

p. 9 - Off to School

p. 16 - Inside on a Rainy Day

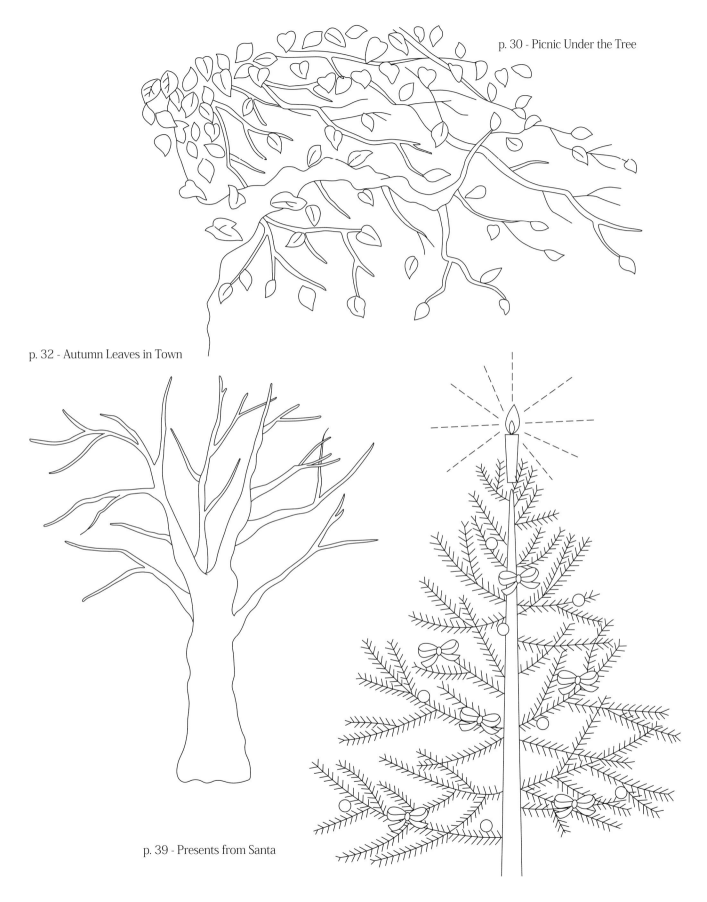

p. 30 - Picnic Under the Tree

p. 32 - Autumn Leaves in Town

p. 39 - Presents from Santa

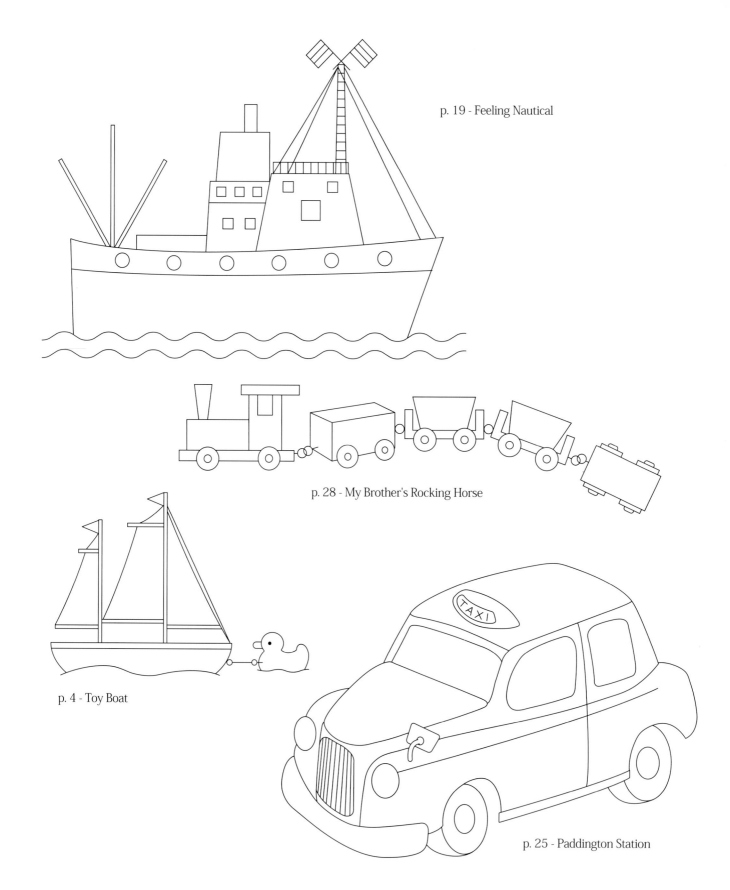

p. 19 - Feeling Nautical

p. 28 - My Brother's Rocking Horse

p. 4 - Toy Boat

p. 25 - Paddington Station

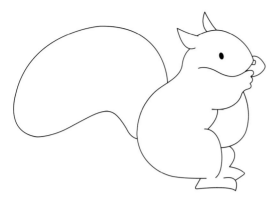

p. 30 - Picnic Under the Tree

p. 19 - Feeling Nautical

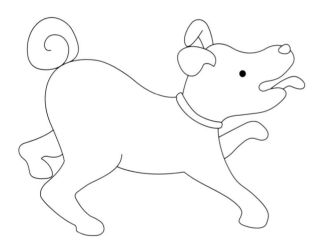

p. 32 - Walking Together

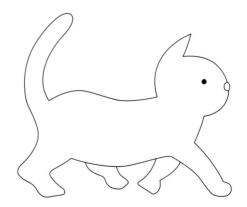

p. 8 - Strolling Along

# Yukari Takahara

Yukari Takahara was born in Kyoto. She graduated from University with a degree in art. In 1992, after teaching in both elementary and middle schools, she and her husband moved back to his hometown. They opened a picture book gallery using their own personal collection. The gallery grew to include a cafe, and a gift and quilt shop called Yuufu-sha. Ms. Takahara teaches crafts and painting from her studio at the same location. In addition to their own art work and activities, they hold many events at Yuufu-sha throughout the year.

Yuufu-sha
154-1 Yanochosakaki, Aioi Shi
Hyogo-Ken, Japan 678-0091

http://www.yufusya (Japanese)

| | | **Staff** | |
| --- | --- | --- | --- |
| Original Title | Story Quilt Kisetsu to tomo ni | Book Design | Mami Shiina |
| Author | Yukari Takahara | Photography | Kazuo Matsushita |
| | ©2007 Yukari Takahara | Editorial Interview | Keiko Nitta |
| First Edition | Originally published in Japan in 2007 | Illustrations | Hiromi Niwano |
| Published by: | Shufu to Seikatsusha | Copyeditor | Takayo Kuriki |
| | 3-5-7 Kyoubashi, Chuo-Ku | Editor | Naoko Akiba |
| | Tokyo, Japan 104-8357 | | |
| | http://www.shufu.co.jp | | |

| | |
| --- | --- |
| Translation | ©2014 Stitch Publications, LLC |
| English Translation Rights | arranged with Stitch Publications, LLC through |
| | Tuttle-Mori Agency, Inc. |
| Published by: | Stitch Publications, LLC |
| | P.O. Box 16694 |
| | Seattle, WA 98116 |
| | http://www.stitchpublications.com |
| Printed & Bound | KHL Printing, Singapore |
| ISBN | 978-0-9859746-9-5 |
| PCN | Library of Congress Control Number: 2014950661 |

This English edition is published by arrangement with Shufu-to-Seikatsusha, through Tuttle-Mori agency, Inc.